Motivational Techniques To Improve Your Team Success

SADANAND PUJARI

Published by SADANAND PUJARI, 2024.

Table of Contents

Copyright 1

About 2

Introduction 3

What Is Motivation 4

The Mind Game Of Motivation 9

What Is De-Motivation 14

Motivation In Your Personal Life 19

Mastering Your Mistakes 22

Misconceptions About Motivation 27

How To Keep Motivated 31

Hero & Villain 36

Conclusion 41

Copyright

Copyright © 2024 by **SADANAND PUJARI**

All rights reserved. No part of this book may be reproduced, scanned, or distributed in any printed or electronic form without permission. Please do not participate in or encourage piracy of copyrighted materials in violation of the author's rights. Purchase only authorized editions.

Motivational Techniques To Improve Your Team Success

Learn Principles & Practices Of Intrinsic Motivators For Team Success; Autonomy, Mastery & Purpose

First Edition: Jun 2024

Book Design by **SADANAND PUJARI**

About

Your success is your ability to motivate and develop your team and team members. If they perform, you perform. This Book will provide those skills that are critical to your success.

Motivation is not a speech or pep talk! It is the skill of creating a worthy purpose, an effective team environment, designing work for intrinsic motivation, and using positive reinforcement in an effective way. This Book will enable you to develop a system of sustained motivation for yourself and your team.

I have authored eleven books and the key to getting books published is simply the self-discipline to sit yourself down and write! I have been CEO of two companies and consulted with more than one hundred major corporations on improving human performance.

In this Book I have distilled the science of human behavior down to the essential practical chapters that every entrepreneur and manager must know and practice to succeed.

Introduction

Motivation is something everyone has inside them. When we wish to do something it's because we are motivated to do so. People invent, discover adventure and interact all due to the motivation inside of them. There are many different things that can motivate you to do something and even not to do something in your life.

The only way to understand motivation is to relate to the situations in which you need it. And that just so happens to be everywhere. There's no person who can claim they've never been motivated to do something good, bad , or selfless selfish.

They're all members of the motivation family and this chapter will take you on a journey where you can find ways to make the best of your motivation.

What Is Motivation

In this chapter we'll discover what motivation is going by the dictionary definition. Motivation is defined as a reason or set of reasons to accomplish something or behave in a particular manner. It's like this driving force we all have which pushes its own pedal when it sees opportunity. For instance when you see an ad for a new job opening and you happen to be looking for something new or different doesn't the voice in the back of your head say why not. And even if you're not looking for something new or different, motivation may just prompt you to ask that very same question. In any case , simply motivation becomes the thriving ambition to have something accomplished in life.

This motivation can help you figure out problems when you're stuck, get over overwhelming emotions and help you aim for new heights. We all have ambitions, dreams and aspirations and the more you allow your motivation to inspire you the more you can get done. It can help you overcome habits as well things like drinking and smoking can stop when you're motivated to see the end of it. Otherwise it's hard to dedicate to something if you do it reluctantly. However with motivation you are driven by a feeling of willingness and inspiration that makes you a lot more ready to take action for or against yourself. Why do you need motivation? There is little debate that motivation is the key to progress.

Everyone must develop their own passions in order to evolve in life. When you want to grow or improve yourself you have to try new things without doing so you won't achieve things such as self recognition and respect which are vital aspects in a healthy life. You may not realize it but you motivate yourself every day. In many small ways for instance right now you've just motivated yourself to read through this chapter. Chances are you're here because you'd like to improve some aspects of your life or on a more generic level. You go to work because there is the motivation of a paycheck at the end of the month. You work hard so that you can earn appreciation and acknowledgement among peers or perhaps the ability to do something that you love motivates you to get up every morning and go to work.

If you have a great boss at work, someone who takes the time to know their employees and appreciates a job well done. Maybe that's what motivates you to go to work and give it your best workplace issues aside. You also motivate yourself in many everyday situations. If you're a giver or someone wishes to help others you may be motivated to donate your time or money to a cause. If you're driven by a desire for achievement you may spend hours studying just to get into a prestigious university. Likewise if self-expression drives you you may be motivated to become a writer or if you're an athlete then perhaps you're driven by the thrill of a sport, the challenge of winning the game or you're simply driven by playing at your personal best.

At its simplest this is what motivation is: it can come from yourself or someone else may push you to do something wherever the source motivation is the initiative to succeed and surpass limits you or anyone else draws for you. There are many situations in which motivation can affect your decisions but they don't all come from the same motivator. Some things require a big step to take action while others like the ones mentioned just need a little shove to get you going. That is the magic of motivation types of motivation in your life. There are different motivators that occur in your life to help you get going. Some motivators are big like quitting a job or moving from one city to another. These motivators get you on your feet for a change almost immediately you're going to need a job.

So you're going to have to look for one as soon as possible. A smaller motivator could be getting a limited time two for one deal at the mall. You may not realize it but at that very moment you've been motivated to take that deal and buy a product. It may be the typical market scam but it's the ideal example of motivation for it gets you to act quickly by setting a time limit on the deal other than big and small motivators there are positive and negative motivators positive motivators are those that inspire you to do something because you know the end result is good. An example could be putting together a baby crib might be a lot of work especially if this is your first attempt but you're still ready to do so because you know you're going to need a bed to place your child in. That proves motivating enough for parents and they willingly assemble the crib for their child.

Being your own boss I mean working 80 hours a week but spares you the hassle of working 40 hours a week for someone else. In other words it gives you the freedom to make your own decisions and work with a feeling of self worth. These are what positive motivators are negative motivators are those things in life that encourage you to do something because you know if you don't do them you'll end up with a bad aftertaste. This doesn't make negative motivators the alternative of a positive motivator though with a positive motivator you act upon it out of free will. However negative motivators are very much needed but you don't do it entirely out of free will.

Deadlines are the best example for this case when you're given a deadline it means that you have to hand work in or face consequences. You don't want to. So the motivator that makes you finish your work on time is to avoid the possible adverse result making it a negative motivator. They can be pesky but sometimes the only way to get things done while all these things motivate. There can also be situations in which they deem motivate you like the third law of Newton for every action there is an equal and opposite reaction motivation and deep motivation. Motivation helps you turn an idea into an action and it's typically a positive feeling. The feeling of accomplishment and commitment and deep motivation is the opposite of this.

It's the perception that you can't accomplish anything or are unable or unfit to and is a gloomy feeling to carry around like a brick pulling down your stomach makes you feel bad and in common cases lethargic deep motivation isn't always in your control a bad day or experience can keep you from doing something about it making you feel bad about yourself. You may have had a horrible experience with driving on your first try and no matter how many times you tried to tell yourself it'll be different the next time you succumb to the failure of the previous time while one person may feel motivated about promotion another may be demotivated by it. The first person here sees it as an ideal opportunity to achieve a higher position and work among colleagues. The second person may feel demotivated because they know their chances at getting that promotion are less than the first person.

This is an example of positive motivation but at the same time it is an unintentional method of demotivating someone else. So while you may feel motivated to bring a crusty Apple to your picnic, someone may feel demotivated by your excellent dessert and not bring their own pie. Sometimes it's out of your control if you do motivate others but sometimes it is and just takes a little consideration to see simply enough. There are times you will be demotivated and it never feels good but unmotivated emotions should never keep you down and instead remind you that there's something to get done. And if you don't do it, who else will do it for you? So the basic idea here is that deep motivation is the countering effect of motivation. It's a block that prevents you from becoming motivated and its cure is if anything.

The Mind Game Of Motivation

In this chapter we'll talk about the mind game of motivation. The concept of motivation isn't a physical one you can't touch motivation as if it were an object to attain. Motivation resembles an emotion or a collection of them that stimulate you to perform an action. It's an aspect of your personality that only you can control and that's why each person can have different motivators and perspectives on what encourages them to do something. Since emotions are the stimulators for your motivation, dealing with your motivators can be sensitive when motivation comes because of an immediate sudden change in a reaction in life. Your emotional response could be blurred to a wrong perspective.

If your motivator took time to develop due to reasoning and thoughtful inquisition you may have a stronger grip and understanding of your motivator as a result. This can yield a stronger and more sensible approach to your newly elated emotions. Where does motivation come from? As mentioned above motivation isn't a physical thing it's easiest to compare to your emotions since they are the main benefactors of your motivation. Depending on how you feel about a certain situation makes the motivation vary from occasion in person. In other words motivation comes from the mind. This is one of the main reasons you could find it really easy or really hard to motivate yourself. But for most motivation doesn't come easy.

It's like a habit and habits are hard to shake off when changing anything about yourself. You'll find that your mentality is the blocking factor to turning into a newer person. If you believe that you deserve the best of the best then it'll be harder to convince or motivate you to do something lower than expectations below yours. If you're more adaptable than finding motivators may be slightly easier. As an open mind finds opportunity more often. Habits like procrastination keeping everything neat or self-consciousness are natural habits people may have with or without realizing it. Things like these that can affect what motivates you.

If you procrastinate then deadlines are probably the only things standing in your way to get something done. And only at the last second. Being neat and orderly could mean that your motivation remains avoiding disaster self-consciousness may motivate you to try and look your best on a daily basis, work out and appear prestigious to everyone. But nobody is born as a motivated person as you develop and become your individual persona. You also develop your perseverance, initiative and sense of responsibility. Since all these qualities combine to make your motivation you also have to have your own motivator chanting in the back of your mind. It may be a strong supportive voice booming in your thoughts all the time that helps you aim for the highest goals you wish to achieve.

It could also be a quiet whistle that likes to ask you feebly what if or why not. Once in a while it may always be there or come along once in a while. It all depends. Essentially motivation is a mind game and the only way to control your motivation is to understand your personality. What makes you you? Answer a question like "What's your view on your own life?" Motivation depends on you. An idea now well-established. So what is it about yourself that motivates you? You may not know it but your whole life up to this moment is built on your motivation. Are you someone who does something because you find it personally rewarding. Or is it because you wish to earn the praise of others.

If you're the first type then you're driven by intrinsic motivation. When something from the inside drives you you end up doing things that you enjoy. That also means that you're less likely to be distracted, you'll feel greater satisfaction in your achievements and be driven by a greater sense of purpose. Alternately if you're pushed by the urge to succeed to gain a specific award or steer clear of a punishment then your motivation is coming from an external source. This is called extrinsic motivation and can be a highly effective motivator on its own. What do you desire in life? Is it self recognition or a grand income? This will determine whether you're the kind of person who'd be motivated by passion and self discovery or business dealings aimed at profiting.

For instance a pet shop owner could be someone passionate about animals or has an experience with them and helps them find families. A manager on the other hand is someone who finds authority a motivator to keep them in charge and in order. They like the higher position in an organization and are capable of taking the heat of sitting on the hot seat. Others may scare from handling animals or buckle under the pressure of authority afraid they won't be able to handle it. So while one person lives to be a leader, someone might enjoy sitting at a safer distance from the chaos where you see yourself is also vital to your motivational strength. Do you feel confident in your own skills or you think they aren't up to par with the others?

Do the opinions of others really matter? Or are you fine turning some heads. Are you fine with what the world has to offer? Or are you ready to hunt down what you feel you deserve. All these factors into what truly motivates you. Your greatest enemy. If you answer these questions you'll come to realize the only thing standing in your way is yourself. Nobody can stop you entirely from being where you need to be or even want to be the only person you have to conquer is yourself. It's hard to change yourself from material habits to your personality while others may say you can do something and invoke you to try new things. Perhaps it's your own thoughts holding you back, feeling insecure about yourself is a main reason why most people don't listen to motivation when doing something new.

Self-doubt keeps you from committing yourself to brighter and unfamiliar endeavors. If you don't feel good about yourself, how are you going to feel good about anything else? Another issue that can often quarrel with motivating yourself to do new things would be ignorance and pride. Some people refuse to mentally open up to new experiences or ideas which means that motivation doesn't encourage them to discover new opportunities but rather stick to their own game. Once again motivation is something each individual has and the idea is that motivation differs from each person based on personal wants and needs.

So while a person believes that going to the beach is a fun idea and would try to go to the beach in their free time. Another might see it as a nuisance to go out and rather motivate themselves to stay at home and enjoy a quiet day indoors. What can make you change yourself is entirely up to you whenever you feel as though you can't pull yourself to do something no one else is stopping you only yourself. Trying new ideas and experiencing unusual things is all progress and self development and can only reap fruitful benefits. That's why when considering something new it's always good to look at the positive side with an open mind. If you can conquer your own emotions then there's nothing standing in your way.

What Is De-Motivation

In this chapter we'll discover what deep motivation is. Deep motivation is the key to being lethargic and unenthusiastic. If you're acquainted with these words you know they don't describe anything near Nice. Motivation acts like a pick me up for most people. Deep motivation is the counter effect to this. Deep motivation keeps you from achieving this. Maybe because of self-doubt or vulnerability, being vulnerable makes you an easier target to discourage words. Some people may have to say the impact of others achievements may make yours seem miniscule which isn't true doesn't stop it from being an achievement it's just your mind toying with you downfalls of remaining demotivated D motivation prevents you from trying out new things when your unmotivated everything seems bigger than you making you feel small and insignificant it's surely not a good feeling and the longer it sticks around the more embedded it becomes.

It's natural to allow something to motivate you for a while. Some people feel that their physical appearance and qualities are what keeps them from achieving. Others believe that they can't operate on a level with the competition and therefore don't even try. Most people just feel that they're too weak to compete with themselves and the change that will follow may be too much to handle. If motivation helps you progress, learn and develop into a better person then it's not hard to figure out what the motivation will do for you. Deep motivation works to counter all that motivation accomplishes for you. That's why you should never let it feel like your system never accepts demotivating thoughts and feelings about yourself. Deep motivation is like a parasite or a virus.

The longer you let it stay the stronger it becomes. If you leave it alone for too long it becomes an irreplaceable part of you. Job opportunities suddenly seem out of your league. Stopping yourself from doing something smoking looks impossible. You accept what you are and not in a positive way. Deep motivation makes you accept that unworthy persona you perceive. Motivation can help you accept the greater you and your possibilities and aspirations. Deep motivation diminishes the light in your character and personality creating a darker and endless cycle of a self indulgent BORING LIFE WITH THE demotivated mind concept you'll never achieve. The hidden full potential you have earned the potential that motivation could have helped you strive for becomes a fading shimmer in the back of your mind too far from your reach and never attainable.

That's why motivation is so important in your life. Getting over deep motivation writers or artists block brain farts and mind stumps whatever you want to call it is hard but not impossible. How to Conquer deep motivation realizing what's demotivating you is the first step. It may be complicated at first deciphering your own actions to realize what's causing them. Talking to a therapist is also a great way to help you understand more about your personality. Deep motivation can come from someone else's words or something you may have seen in past experiences. You may simply lack the required enthusiasm to commit to anything. It's normal and possible to conquer.

Talking is the best way to realize that there's a block in your mind preventing you from taking bigger stronger steps. Once you've figured out what's keeping you down you can take steps to write it out of your life. One great step to do is get out of your comfort zone. Go see new things and talk to people about secrets you've never shared. Trusting someone with your struggles, someone you know would never leave you a helping hand is always better when you're trying to climb a mountain on your own though they don't have the same mind as yours. They can help strengthen yours with advice and support.

Even if one person can help. It's enough after finding help you can create a list of all the things you want to do. Even if some of those ideas seem crazy they're your ambitions and they're nothing to be ashamed of having your list somewhere you can see it every day on the bathroom mirror in the kitchen or even on your bedroom door somewhere you know it's going to be always in your face reminding you that it's there a reminder of the things you want to do can help trigger motivation in your heart. Ask your trustworthy friend to push you around, take you to new places and even try going to new areas on your own small steps like taking a walk every morning or having a new drink every day can encourage the most nation of flame in your heart until you have a fire. Why let yourself remain demotivated?

The biggest reason is simply because it's the easier way out. Even though you know that staying demotivated is never going to get things done some people actually want this to be the case. There are multiple reasons behind why some people feel being demotivated is OK. Remaining demotivated to pick up your pieces and make a change means that no change will ever come.

Later on we discuss why change is a big step that's needed. But the fact is that some people are afraid of change. No one can be entirely sure what's going to happen when change comes around the corner. If you decide not to do anything about the way your life is going then who is. Some people enjoy the idea of not having to move on and stay right where they are. What you may not realize is that while you're relaxing in your own bubble those around you are stuck alongside you.

They may have to stay put. Since you refuse to move. Another reason is a little more serious than staying in your safety bubble. Some people just don't have the motivation in them unmotivated and motivated emotions are constantly combating against one another. If you don't have any motivation then what's going to tamper down all of your demotivated emotions. D motivation is easy. Some people can even be considered champions and abuse the love that Jack has for doing nothing all the time. They will put the blame on everything and everyone else for why they don't do things they will suffice on what they have and never move. They will also never achieve anything in life.

It may sound fun not having to do anything that goes out of the way for you but there's also the frustration of never accomplishing never truly understanding what you're worth. People who follow passions and ambitions with a full heart and high hopes realize they are worth their value. Never leaving the box means that your only value will remain in that box. Nothing. No one out of your scheduled area will ever realize or discover the potential you wield. And that's just not something worth risking. Whether it's fear or carelessness that keeps a person down in the dust, motivated hearts will always be stronger than demotivated ones.

Motivation In Your Personal Life

In this chapter we'll talk about motivation in your personal life. Everyone has their own life happening amongst others. The easiest thing that you can do is focus on yourself and sometimes that's fine. The more you learn about yourself the easier it will become to allow others into your life. One reason a person may avoid interaction is because they're unsure and insecure about themselves and therefore scared of not knowing who they are when others are around seeing confident people walk with our tour understanding and completion makes those who don't have that feel wary. One way to truly understand who you are is by recollecting every emotion you feel and what it sparks in your actions.

What is your motive? Every day we're motivated everyday by something in the morning you get up, shower , eat change and go to work. You may say it's routine but the question is what's compelling you to do all of this. The answer is simple and clear. Motivation: you're motivated to smell nice and keep clean before being around other people. Otherwise people will be able to smell your last meal on your breath. You eat because you know you have to survive. It's a must and so you motivate yourself to eat at least before going to work to get it out of the way. You're motivated to change because you don't want to feel undermined wearing the same smelly clothes you sleep in at night around your peers every day all day. We make subconscious choices because they have become a habit. If someone were to ask you why you brush your teeth, what would you say?

Because I have to be the first dancer to pop into your mind. But ask yourself the same question again: Why do you brush your teeth every day? It's because you know that teeth can be damaged if you don't clean them. Do you want to have a perfect smile or are you scared of having teeth that others don't like? What motivates you personally to keep your teeth clean. And for how many times a day personal development when you motivate yourself you move forward. There's no going back once you've made a choice and motivation tries to make sure the step you took was the largest step you could take with your own individual personalities.

You want to move to a final destination and then possibly further as you make steps you as a person develop further into a persona someone may feel something you've never felt. Doing something you would never do and not understanding why is the most frustrating thing in the world. That's why you want to become more known and understand more. There's no top to reach but there's always higher. What everyone wants is to see how high they can go and where they find a place they can proudly fit into. This is personal development. We want to change. We want to survive and we want to please those we know who we don't. And most importantly ourselves to become a better person.

We have to understand what it means to be a person and that only happens when we stick out our necks venturing into the real system and manage to show you what the world has to offer. This is what makes us whole and why you strive for more. There is no exact reason for why one person wants to endure the hardships of moving forward; everyone will work differently from another person. Tactics to the top won't be the same for others. Trickery and lies can get one person to achieve where they want to be. Being the kind helping hand and supportive friend will earn another person a gravitated name. Most people want recognition realizing what you live for is a hard question to answer and the truth is there is no affirmed answer that can be handed to you. The answer for this question lies in each individual's own character.

Whomever it comes from so long as it comes to us we feel there is something worth doing. One person enjoys helping others over themselves. Another wants to make a statement. All will listen to what you do to help others and what your statement is depends on you. The fact is you eventually want the result. The final reaction no one stops until they get what satisfies them satisfaction is the key to knowing your motivation paid off to make you who you are. As long as someone can still stand with us or ahead of us we will keep moving forward. Similar to a Rolling Stone. There is no other way to go besides forward.

Mastering Your Mistakes

In this chapter we'll talk about mastering your mistakes, motivation and drive are all great but it's important to remember that mistakes will be made on the way. This is something everyone experiences and dreads at the same time. Some learn from their mistakes never letting them come in the way of their motivation while others get derailed. Everyone fears mistakes and the main reason is judgment. Everyone fears being judged by those superior to them and near them. The truth is it's okay to be judged on the one condition that you believe in yourself. You made a mistake and you can attain it , accept it and admit to it. Your decisions are yours to make and make you who you are. If you don't make your own decisions you'll never truly be your own person.

Other people can manipulate, encourage and influence you but it's the decision you take afterwards that makes you an individual. If this seems too inspiring. Think of baby steps. If an infant were to never fall over while trying to walk it would never develop the fear of falling or the love of standing properly without collapsing. Collapsing shows them what happens if you walk without balance and they seek to conquer that in order to walk like everyone else does no matter what age you are. Motivation drives us to grow and mistakes are the stepping stones to success along the road. Change in every step with every choice you make there's going to be change and change can bring along mistakes just as well mistakes can bring along change to clear it up.

A great example would be walking down a new path rather than going down the same one you do every day. You take a new one. First comes the power of motivation. After going down the same path every day it does get a little boring. Now you figured out that a different path leads to your same destination and you have access to it. It may be longer and may be shorter. It's up to you to find out this act of motivation to discover is going to bring along change. You'll see new things while you walk. You'll see the environment familiar with it and see new faces along the way. You may even make mistakes while you do any simple innocent mistake like tripping on a crack you didn't know was there. Locals to the neighborhood may not make this mistake because they knew but you didn't and so came to be your blunder.

This is what change can offer. Change brings with it. Experience knowledge and development. If you can surpass all the inevitable mistakes, mistakes are nothing to be ashamed of. And change should never be feared. One thing people can't seem to shake is that change is like a back alley in the dead of night. You don't know what awaits in the end. This can definitely make change seem intimidating. There are larger cases than walking down a new road like walking down a new world in a different country. It's a completely different group of people around you with different expectations, different surroundings and different mentalities.

You definitely don't want to trip over any cracks here but you may and who said anything about it. Now you know you're familiarizing yourself with change. A new place and people and they're not new anymore. You know more and understand more by walking down the back alley and suddenly it isn't so dark. How mistakes can help you. Mistakes can bring along change just like change does mistakes. They are a continuous cycle that helps you make progress to improve yourself. Going back to your walk when you walk down the new path and stumbled over the crack you'll learn something. Now you know there is a crack in the sidewalk and the next round you'll watch out for it.

This mistake taught you something. And next time you won't make that mistake. Learning from the mistakes so that you won't do it again brought about change. This change is going to help you in not making the same mistakes so you can keep going down that road. You may even start paying more attention to the road from this time forward which is another change brought forth by the mistake you made. Had you not gone down that road you would have never stumbled and learned that there are crevices down the sidewalk meaning you never developed the awareness of it. Tripping over a crack is such an insignificant thing to do but there's a lot behind the action that occurs afterwards. That's why you can never overlook your mistakes. They are chapters in disguise but the real question is what started this adventure down a dented sidewalk.

The little rush of motivation you got to walk down the road is what made this possible without motivation to do things. We are nothing without the mistakes we make. We will never learn that an inventor makes a faulty machine that doesn't work. Business man makes a sales choice that doesn't sell. A mother decides to make a new dish that doesn't turn out to be five stars. All these actions turned out to be less than perfect but that still means the inventor felt motivated to make the machine. The businessman felt motivated to make new sales and the mother wanted to try new recipes. Now they all know better due to their mistakes and make a choice based on it. Will they accept defeat and never try again or learn from the mistake and try once more to do something new and creative evolution is based on mistakes and mistakes should never be.

What motivates you. No pain no gain. Mistakes mean you take the fall. If you do something wrong accidentally or on purpose for the sake of curiosity you've made a mistake. Now it's up to you to learn from it or avoid it. A mistake must be admitted before you can ever learn something from it. It's not a mistake to do something on purpose with the means of inflicting harm. That's plainly being rebellious and crude. A mistake means no harm and is something to learn from. If an inventor never made a mistake because they feared the idea of it how would they ever learn to move ahead from the mistake. Fear is a natural reaction to most things that involve new aspects in life. Mistakes open new possibilities, new doors and sharpen who you are, which some people don't want.

Taking the initiative to make a change and understand that mistakes will be made along the way is one part of the whole story. The next part is admitting to that mistake. It can be embarrassing. It can be terrifying. These feelings come from your stifled influence from others around you. The only thing you need to know is that the only opinion that matters is yours. This is your mistake and no one can take it back. Hearing words from others can only help you so much. It's what you do to yourself that matters in the end. Welling up around the mistake and letting it taunt you isn't a profitable way to take things.

Admitting, accepting and learning from it are the real actions you'll benefit from. Once you lead in the mistake you can gain from it. What did you learn and how can you overcome making that mistake again? The saying is true without any pain. There will never be anything to gain.

Misconceptions About Motivation

In this chapter we'll discuss misconceptions about motivation. Believe it or not there are wrong ways to approach motivation but once again you can always learn from the mistakes you make. Since motivation comes from the mind it is possible to over think motivation but motivation isn't something you have to conquer in order to achieve it. Motivation comes naturally similar to adrenaline. It's not as powerful as adrenaline doesn't leak out when you're in danger or excited. Instead it's always there for you as an encouraging hand to pat your back. It isn't mandatory either to feel as though you must always be motivated. You can always take a break from the motivation of doing something extravagant and submit to being tired. Taking a rest or break from pursuing something gives you time to prepare for the next wave of motivation you may have.

But people tend to read motivation wrong. Here are some common misconceptions surrounding motivation. You are alone. It may appear so but you are never alone. You can always ask someone for help or advice on how to do something with a world of seven point five billion people and escalating it shouldn't be hard to find one person in which you can confide in. Everyone has their own perspective and sometimes it helps to get a second opinion when you need a push. You can always ask someone else for a helping hand. Personal projects may mean that yes you have to act on your own but you can always ask for advice, tips or favors from other people. A problem most people have is that they feel there's no one for them.

Family friends and coworkers are too far away from reach and so they don't see any shoulder to turn to. The truth is most people are happy to help. It's a natural instinct to try and help when you see an infant. Don't you want to cradle it and tuck it in the sheet so that it stays warm. It's instinct to help out no matter how reluctant you may make yourself out to be, providing some kind of support isn't hard. Even if it's just a consoling word, never feel as though nobody has your back because people are always going to be there for you. So as long as you can do the same for them.

This doesn't mean that every favor you do is an eye for an eye. It simply means that when someone's in need of help feel free to lend out a hand out of kindness they may be more willing to lend a hand to you later on when you need it. Of course it takes a different motivation on its own to approach people or a person to commune with them. But interaction is natural. Loneliness makes you sad and an introvert going out of your way to get to know people and make friends is a good thing. And like all things requires a little encouragement you need Push to shove you don't quite need someone to push you into doing something you can do anything. When your heart truly desires you just need to see it. Some people feel that change needs to occur first in order for anything enticing to happen to them.

This isn't entirely true. It's true that change does mean something different has to happen. When change occurs you motivate yourself to keep up with the shifting world around you because you have to likewise change doesn't necessarily have to come first. Motivation can sometimes be the push to encourage change. It's easier to put the blame on something else rather than admit to your own faults. People often say that nothing ever happens in their boring lives so they have nothing to do. Is this really what goes on? Or do we often ignore our ambitious selves constantly wiring ourselves to the realistic perspective. Usually this is the case that we avoid our own thoughts of motive inspirations and accept that they can't be achieved. Doing this. You are on the one way train to sadness days will slowly become meaningless all because you were waiting for a push to come and shove you to your feet.

If you can't stand on your own two feet, who's going to do it for you? That which leads us on is already built inside us and is called motivation. Motivation is the push we shove ourselves with to get things done. The only people in charge of our lives are us, not those around pointing fingers and directing orders. Take those orders if you must but don't let them stop you from pushing yourself to your maximum capability. You need motivation for big steps. You need motivation for any step by staying motivated. You take each and every step you need in order to reach the coffee machine sitting in the kitchen. You drive as far as you need to go to get to your office because you are motivated to get to work. Nobody can see just how important motivation is because we take advantage of it every day.

It's the voice telling us what time it is where we need to be because these are daily motivators that keep us moving. We don't even realize when they are acting in our mind because they work so silently. We only take account of our motivation when we're trying to push ourselves to do something out of the way. It's like there's a running motor in our minds but bricks on the feet something out of your daily behavior requires a little more motivation. If you want to do anything your motivation is already set into action. Go to the library to get a book, grab a coffee with your friends and shop for a new outfit. They all mean that motivation is driving you forward.

If you've ever felt lethargic or seen someone who was then you've seen what life without motivation would look like you wouldn't be able to see past the work to the reward afterwards. Getting up would seem like too much work and doing work would seem too much of a bother. No motivation means there's no ambition, passion or final result to look forward to. Why would you bother doing anything knowing you aren't going to get anything from it? That is what it feels like without motivation and it never feels good when you recall what motivation does for you each and every day. Consider how much you achieve daily. Imagine an animal out in the wild with no straight idea of what will happen in the day and if they will live another one.

Humanity has developed to such an extent that we can finally predict the outgoings of our days from months even years to come. You're part of that system where you fit in a flow in a vast line of coordinated actions to continue the man made balance in a cruel world. If that isn't enough to make you smile then remember no one can take the place you've made for yourself in the world and no one can live your life better than you can. Everything needs motivation. A smile means you move your muscles. Travelling means you take initiative to work out your plan and involve yourself. Nothing is left unturned when you're motivated.

How To Keep Motivated

In this chapter we'll discover how you can keep yourself motivated. Being a motivated person is one step. Everyone crosses or still needs to know how to make sure you remain motivated in life though it is an entirely different situation. Sustaining that ignition to keep fueling your own fire isn't as easy as throwing logs into a fireplace. Since you're working with the Mind here Those logs are emotions and ambitions and the smoke should be your several thoughts of doubt going out the chimney. There are many ways people try to keep themselves motivated and reminded of the tasks to accomplish. A personal favorite would be the rubber band around the arm.

Unfortunately you can only snap at yourself so many times before it starts hurting and you forget that the band is even there when you try to stay motivated. You have to think of the long term plan. There's a lot to face in life and new things will always splash over your plate. To keep motivated you have to be able to wash your plate off in order to serve what you want. Prioritize. Look through all the plans you have and see which ones need to be done first. This could mean giving the house a new coat of paint. Making a doghouse or playpen. Long term plans such as going on vacation can wait for another time. Material matters affecting the present are what you should focus more on.

Keep in mind anything that is long term you can prepare for now while you're working on something else but not as a top priority. Only when things in future terms become the present do they get the benefit of being prioritized to make these simpler smaller tasks should be done first. So they're out of the way. Register yourself for a language class or into a gym. These small commitments can be done first so that they're out of the way. The most relatable example should be losing weight once in everyone's life. People have thought of working on their physical bodily appearance, prioritizing this means any other long term projects will have to be for later.

Since this requires your full attention, just 20 minutes is what you need to start yourself off. Nobody can start working out like a weightlifting champion. Still if you have other concerns on your mind you may slip and forget working out as a priority. Once you get the workouts rooted into your schedule you can try applying any other long term plans into your day. Other things such as equipment and the change in diet are things you do before you even start working out. Prioritize buying the essential equipment you need and swapping carbs and empty calories for healthy ripe fruits and all natural homemade shakes.

Planning your steps when motivation is paired with planning it becomes a sure fire formula for winning. Continuing with the example of losing weight the next step would be to plan out your steps to exploit your agenda. Planning out your steps may mean by a day to day basis or you can make a weekly plan. The first thing to do is find empty spaces inside your routine. Make room for your daily fitness activities so that you can make routine with your workouts. In other cases besides this one. Figure out how much time your activity would take and find that much consecutive time in your schedule. After you find the time for all these things, start with baby steps. Do the simplest version of what you want to do in order to introduce yourself to your new hobby.

For workouts it would be the simplest cardio workout to get the feeling of what you're getting yourself into next while you get the hang of your new hobby activity. Try adding more time and challenge to your daily session making it more interesting. Keep at it until you finally have it rooted in your daily routine. Other objectives like making plans take time and planning to. First comes the research and then the action to prepare for the plan. The same strategy would apply for planning, say a vacation. The only difference here would be rather than making it more challenging. You get closer to your goal day by day until you finally reach the goal. Planning for something other than a hobby means that you aren't going to pursue it. Once it's achieved, there's no need to keep holding onto it.

Instead what you want to do is get it done as soon as possible so that it doesn't linger where you don't need it. Keep this in mind when you differentiate between possible hobbies and simple one time plans. When you've got your plans laid out everything else naturally falls in line. Keep on track once you've got the blueprint on how you're going to pursue this hobby or plan. It comes down to your own initiative to keep yourself going. Making a plan is much easier than sticking to the plan for some people which is why this is the hardest part. Remove yourself from any activity until you've gotten a hold of the first one. If you try working out and suddenly you decide you're going to practice ice skating, that's going to take away from your dedication to losing weight. You've got distracted and now going back means returning to square one which can discourage people quite easily.

No side dedications focus on what you need to do making a plan for the holidays means you stick to those plans and work on them beforehand. Not in the vacations preplan and finish planning as soon as you can do that. So there's no procrastination and last minute changes it's hard dedicating to something and making it a habit. You may think of giving up some time along the road but there's always time to get back up and try again. Life has a meaning and it never hurts to keep yourself going to find it in the end. Knowing when you've made something habit comes naturally. Sooner or later you'll find yourself automatically taking yourself to the gym or lifting weights at home because it's become a natural reaction to having free time.

By then you'll know that you've achieved what you wanted and you can move to something new if that's what you want. Rewarding yourself there are no exceptions for this one. Everyone deserves to feel accomplished even if all you did was stop a bad habit or start a better one. Everyone accomplishes things on their own levels. Each level is a new step for self development and who has the right to overlook that. When you achieve your goals. Celebrating gaining that ideal you wanted means a lot. Rewarding yourself makes you feel good about yourself and that strengthens your morale. This means that you increase confidence and by extension more motivation to achieve. These are all stepping stones to increasing your motivation and self-respect.

The more aware you become of what you can do makes you feel and behave like a better person. Take your achievements modestly and don't let pride consume the best of your accomplishments. Anything can be rewarded and if you stopped smoking then you deserve to announce it. Make yourself and others proud. If you learn a new language traveled to enunciate your new skills no one deserves to feel prouder than you. You need to realize that you're capable of exceeding the limits drawn by your own hand or the hand of others.

Hero & Villain

In this chapter we'll talk about motivation, the hero and the villain. The final prospect to understand about motivation is that it doesn't only encourage you to do something but may encourage you to not do something as well. It can help you overcome fears and blocks while also being the foundation to some other ones. Motivation helps you thrive off of the Kick It has to offer but sometimes that kick isn't forward it's backward. It isn't always a bad thing to take a step back. Sometimes your motivation ensures your firm on staying away from dangerous and harmful things motivating yourself to do something. When you motivate yourself to do something it's something you yearn for. You're willing to try and accomplish what you thrive for. Motivation pushes you towards what you want to do.

Motivating yourself to do something means that you run towards the goal and your motivation pushes you in order to get there what you want is good for you and you get it for your own benefit. It may seem confusing to see the line between motivation towards and against an act or behavior. So let's explore it in further depth. There's an act of motivation where you're being pushed towards something and then the act of being pulled or pushed away from another. Motivating yourself to do something could be learning a new language. You do have something to gain from this and therefore you endure towards it.

You want to learn and develop a new skill so you drive yourself to the finish line and once you have the new skill you have it for the rest of your life. Motivating yourself away from something means you pull yourself away from an actor's behavior. If you commonly get angry or agitated and seek to control it you're going to motivate yourself to get away from the emotion or anger trying to make anger one of your last resorts rather than first means you're pulling out of that regular habit of yours. Once you get accustomed to using other primary emotions then forever you want to try and direct yourself away from the anger you wield.

In this case you're running away from your behaviors or actions rather than approaching them. This is the difference between motivation pushing you and pulling you. Sometimes it's better to run away or leave something rather than embrace its improper nature. Motivation can help you do both push and pull and in your best intentions motivating yourself to not do something before indulging into this theory. It's first vital to understand the deep motivation and motivation working against an action are different. At times it may seem like the same description and definition but motivating yourself is indefinitely not the same thing as demotivating yourself demotivating yourself towards something means that there's no willingness towards performing that specific or even any act at all.

When you're demotivated you wish to do something but your emotions and thoughts convince you that you can't do it no matter how much you hunger for it. When your motivation stands against an act or behavior it means you willingly avoid it with pursuit. You don't want to do something because it stands against what you believe in so your motivation assists you in dodging the bullet. So when you compare the two hand in hand, deep motivation rid you of any willingness to act while motivating yourself against something allows your willingness to act contrary to this action. Motivation still pushes you to do what you want in this case, only it's pushing you away. Deep motivation will be applied in a case where you want to do or have something but you feel unaccomplished or capable of doing or getting it.

Take smoking as an easy to understand example when someone wishes to stop smoking there are two ways they could go about it. One would be that they feel incapable of giving it up although they know that there's a way to fight it. They don't feel proficient enough to make it to the end and surrender. This is deep motivation no matter how much you try your own self works against you making you slouch and lack the drive to pursue your ambition a different road to go down would be making it all the way to the end where you can finally stop smoking. This is the strength of your motivation pushing you away from smoking making sure you never do that again once you've stopped motivation against something it's still motivation.

Only this time the push you get is to pull you out of a bad situation or place. Once you've figured out what's keeping you down you could take steps to writing it out of your life. One great step to do is get out of your comfort zone. Motivating yourself to stay away from bad people or away from dangerous areas are examples of motivation pulling you out instead of pushing you in. Why do you think we avoid our fear so well? It's because we're motivated by the importance of pros and cons when making any decision. It's always better in nature that you consider all the pros and cons that may follow any action. There's always a side to the story and to make sure no one gets hurt from your choice.

Considering the bigger picture is key to making wiser choices, something you consider to be fun and well for you may affect others around you. If you feel as though you prefer going out every night rather than staying at home. Think of both sides of the story. There's your story and what you gain from it then what others gain or lose from it. For you it means you get to go out and have fun with friends, maybe enjoy the outdoors or go to a club that is all fun and games for your side of the story. These would be the pros: the friends you go out with are also having a great time with you, making every night a blast for their side of the story. This would also be a pro to wrap it up. You all get to enjoy time together which makes everything even better. Then there are the people at home. They aren't enjoying the fun and games instead staying home at night.

They could be upset that you aren't there. They could feel left out or even worried about where you go every night. For them this would be a con. This should also affect you as a con since the people in your home are part of your responsibility if they're worried about you that means you're creating a rift between you and your home. If you consider all these together before making a choice you can make an educated decision much better than rationally acting on instinct. The best move to make here is create coordinated plans that everyone can agree on. House members can easily work without you when leaving on a certain day and these nights out don't happen every night to satisfy everyone.

Try including as many people so that these nights don't make anyone feel excluded or make it up to those who don't go. People typically give into peer pressure with the motivation of getting accepted socially. This may lead to them making choices which are not in their nature but they only do so to gain acceptance in social circles. Some kids may start to bully others take up smoking or substance use just to appear cool, driven by the desire to become accepted. There are pros and cons in all our choices. Most of the time we're not in control of how someone else is going to see these choices. They might think of it as a bad idea while you don't. We have to make do with the best that we can do making sure that as many choices we have control over have pros outnumbering the cons.

Conclusion

The evolution of your own personality comes from the motivation that makes you strive to become a better person. Change comes along for the ride whenever we unearth alluring possibilities. Mistakes have to be made in order for you to learn how to stand when we fall even after it all. Nothing will beat the feeling of having accomplished your goals when it's all over you know that your motivation paid off in the end. Making your experience a fruitful one whether it keeps you going or prevents you from doing something silly. Motivation is there to help you accomplish it will help you clear your mind and show you what you really desire out of life and all of its tosses and turns sharp corners leading to new roads and experiences. Motivation has got your back.

www.ingramcontent.com/pod-product-compliance
Lightning Source LLC
Chambersburg PA
CBHW072054230526
45479CB00010B/1066